Marriage GOD'S WAY:

— INSPIRED BY GOD —

DOROTHY L. STARKS

WESTBOW
PRESS®
A DIVISION OF THOMAS NELSON
& ZONDERVAN

WestBow Press books may be ordered through booksellers or by contacting:

WestBow Press
A Division of Thomas Nelson & Zondervan
1663 Liberty Drive
Bloomington, IN 47403
www.westbowpress.com
844-714-3454

Scripture quotations taken from The Holy Bible, New International Version® NIV®
Copyright © 1973 1978 1984 2011 by Biblica, Inc. TM. Used by permission. All rights reserved worldwide.
will send email once outlook starts working again.

ISBN: 978-1-6642-0350-1 (sc)
ISBN: 978-1-6642-0349-5 (e)

Print information available on the last page.

WestBow Press rev. date: 09/04/2020

To Pastor Bradley and Pastor Bea Bacon for teaching me the Word of God and living godly lives.

Psalm 139:1–14

O LORD, YOU HAVE SEARCHED ME AND YOU KNOW ME
YOU KNEW WHEN I SIT AND WHEN I RISE
YOU PERCEIVE MY THOUGHTS FROM AFAR
YOU DISCERN MY GOING OUT AND MY LYING DOWN; YOU ARE
FAMILIAR WITH ALL MY WAYS. BEFORE A WORD IS ON MY TONGUE
YOU KNOW IT COMPLETELY, O LORD YOU HEM ME IN—BEHIND AND
BEFORE, YOU HAVE LAID YOUR HAND UPON ME.

SUCH KNOWLEDGE IS TOO WONDERFUL FOR ME
TOO LOFTY FOR ME TO ATTAIN
WHERE CAN I GO FROM YOUR SPIRIT?
WHERE CAN I FLEE FROM YOUR PRESENCE?
IF I GO UP TO THE HEAVENS, YOU ARE THERE
IF I MAKE MY BED IN THE DEPTHS YOU ARE THERE
IF I RISE ON THE WINGS OF THE DAWN
IF I SETTLE ON THE FAR SIDE OF THE SEA, EVEN THERE YOUR HAND
WILL GUIDE ME, YOUR RIGHT HAND WILL HOLD ME FAST.

IF I SAY, SURELY THE DARKNESS WILL HIDE ME AND THE LIGHT
BECOME NIGHT AROUND ME, EVEN THE DARKNESS WILL NOT BE
DARK TO YOU, THE NIGHT WILL SHINE LIKE THE DAY, FOR DARKNESS
IS AS LIGHT TO YOU:

FOR YOU CREATED MY INMOST BEING; YOU KNIT ME TOGETHER IN
MY MOTHER'S WOMB
I PRAISE YOU BECAUSE I AM FEARFULLY AND WONDERFULLY MADE
YOUR WORKS ARE WONDERFUL I KNOW THAT FULL WELL.

Remember that God loves you unconditionally and knows all about you.

Chapter One
READY TO GET MARRIED?

So you are ready to get married. You have found a special someone you think you want to spend the rest of your life with—the one who makes you laugh, the one who calls you pretty, the one who says he loves you and whom you can't live without.

I just want to ask you a few questions. Do you and your mate have God in your life? Is God the most important thing in your life? Do you want the kind of marriage God has planned for you? If so, then let's look at what God says about marriage.

The Word of God pictures marriage as an institution of God. We should talk about this with our young people, particularly with those who are preparing for their wedding days and lives as married couples. The Lord God brought the woman to the man and with his hand brought unto every man his wife. God has instituted marriage.

This scriptural way of speaking about marriage tells of how serious scripture is to be taken when we as Christians prepare for marriage. God's Word has been looked down on as being narrow-minded, old-fashioned, and judgmental. This is important. We know that scripture speaks about marriage as an institution of God, and we wish to hold on to the truth. We need to submit ourselves to God's Word.

As Christians, we are to take a stand against the contemporary notion that all kinds of institutions in practice in society have merely evolved during the course of history. We are to take a stand against any society that regards any situation other than the institution of marriage as the union of one man and one female "for as long as you both shall live" as the institution to be confessed and practiced in marriage. With God's hand, bring unto every man his wife. God is our Father, the Creator of heaven and earth, who has instituted marriage.

This institution of God is characterized by a common bond to be regarded as a creation order. God created man after his image, but at the same time, God created "male and female." He created them in such a way that husband and wife are meant for each other and predisposed to complete each other in marriage.

Chapter Two
MARRIAGE: THE INSTITUTED

Marriage was instituted in paradise when man was innocent (Gen. 2:18–24.) Here we have its original charter, which was confirmed by our God, as the basis on which all regulations are to be framed (Matt. 19:5; 1 Cor. 6:16). This law was violated when corrupt usage began (Gen. 4:19; 6–2). Marriage is to be between man and woman. This is God's law.

It seems to happen in the practice from the beginning that two fathers selected wives for their sons (Gen. 24:3; 38:6), although sometimes proposals were instituted by the fathers of the maidens (Ex. 2–21). The brothers of maidens were also sometimes consulted (Gen. 24:51; 34:11), but the maidens' own consent was not required. The young man was required to give a price (a dowry) to the father of the maiden (Ex. 31:15; 34:12; 22:16–17; 1 Sam. 18:23, 25; Ruth 4:10; Hos. 3:2) under these patriarchal customs of Mosaic Law.

In the pre-Mosaic times, when the proposal was accepted and the marriage price was given, the bridegroom could come at once and take his bride to his house (Gen. 24:63–67). But in general, the marriage was celebrated by a feast in the house of the bride's parents, to which all friends were invited (Gen. 29:22–27). And on the day of the marriage, the bride, concealed under a thick veil, was conducted to her future husband's home.

God corrected many false notions that existed on the subject of marriage (Matt. 22:23–30) and placed it as a divine institution on the highest grounds. The apostles stated clearly and enforced the nuptial duties of husband and wife (Eph. 5:22–23; Col. 3:18–19; 1 Pet. 3:1, 7).

Marriage is said to be "honorable" (Heb. 13:4), and the prohibition of it is noted as one of the marks of degenerated times (1 Tim. 4:3).

The marriage relationship is used to represent the union between God and these people (Isa. 45:5; Jer. 3:1–4; Hos. 2:9, 20). In the New Testament, the same figure is employed to represent the love of Christ to his saints (Eph. 5:25–27). The church of the redeemed is the "Bride, the Lamb's wife" (Rev. 19:7–9).

Chapter Three
DO YOU WANT THE KIND OF MARRIAGE THAT GOD WANTS FOR YOU?

I hope you do! Let's look at the relationship God wants for his people. That great love that God has for us. Doing God's will whatever the cost.

Let's look at a story in God's Word about a marriage: love finds a way.

The bridegroom is Boaz (Ruth 4). Boaz had a job to do and knew he could find his relative at the town gate. The law of the kinsman-redeemer is given in Leviticus 25:23–24, and the law governing levirate marriage is found in Deuteronomy 24:5–10. The purpose of these laws was to preserve the name and protect the property in Israel.

God owned the land and didn't want it exploited by rich people who would take advantage of poor people, including widows. When obeyed, theses law made sure that a dead man's family name did not die with him and that his property was not sold outside the tribe or clan. The tragedy is the Jewish ruler didn't always obey this law.

Boaz cleverly presented his case to the relative. First, he brought in new information not yet mentioned in the story: Elimelech, Naomi's deceased husband, still had some property in the area that was now for sale. As the relative, this man had the first right to buy the land, which he agreed to do (Lev. 25:25). But Boaz said that according to the law, if the relative bought the property, he also had to marry the widow. Mahlon was Ruth's former husband and Elimelech's son had inherited the property. At this stipulation, the relative backed down. He did not want to complicate his inheritance. He may have feared that if he had a son through Ruth, some of his estate would transfer away from his family to the family of Elimelech.

Boaz was undoubtedly relieved when his relative stepped aside and opened the way for Ruth to become his wife. It's worth noting that the kinsman tried to protect his name and inheritance. Boaz took the risk of love and obedience, and his name is written down in scripture and held in honor. "He who does the will of God abides forever" (John 2:17).

You see, being obedient and having the love of God lets things happen for the good. God has a plan for us (Jer. 29:11). Please take time and read the book of Ruth. There is more to the story.

I want you to think of unconditional love that we find in 1 Corinthians 13. This chapter of the Bible gives us a beautiful definition of real love, as does John 3:16. God shows what real love is: when you can lay down your life for someone else.

We know that it's the Lord's will for his people to have a mate if they desire one. In the beginning, God created Adam. God made this statement: "It is not good that man should be alone; I will make him a help mate for him."

Chapter Four
WALKING IN LOVE UNCONDITIONALLY

Have you ever found yourself irritated with your mate, not liking him or her very much even though you know you love him or her? Most of us have had those days. It's perfectly normal. No two people can live together for any length of time without once in a while rubbing each other the wrong way.

What's important is how you end these kinds of times. If you let those feelings hurt or disappointment takes over, your marriage will suffer. You will create upset in your relationship. So you have to make a choice; you have to decide to love. You may not feel like loving, but if you decide to love, your feelings will follow.

You have to learn to demonstrate unconditional love to your mate. Unconditional love is necessary for strong marriages. Here are some questions to consider.

1. Have you accepted your mate's failures and weaknesses?
2. Do you support your mate? Do you see his or her weakness as a project to fix?
3. Are you afraid to be honest because your mate might not accept you?

There is a huge difference between unconditional love and conditional love. Condition blames a person, expects things in return, and asks for more. Unconditional love accepts the person and expects nothing in return in sacrifice. First Corinthians 13:4–7 tells us how to love, love is patient, how to be patient with our mates, how love is kind, and how to say good things about our mates and to be kind and gentle with them. First Peter 3:5 tells women to submit themselves to their husbands, and if they are more spiritual than the men, they can win them over by the words that come from their mouths. (I know this works.) If you want to see changing in your home, speak great thing about your mate. God said to love as he does, and that is unconditionally.

The Lord wants to bless marriage unions and see his plan fulfilled in both mates' lives. God's plan from the beginning for both male and female is to trust him in this important decision one's life. If you are totally willing to commit to do his will, you will never be disappointed in the one God sends into your life.

Your life reflects God; you are to show the world how God does things. Continue to pray and read God's word daily. And show God's love daily.

The Lord wants to bring a mate to those who will ask him and have the patience to wait. There are some single people who are constantly looking for a mate, and they are miserable. God has not sent them yet. They have prayed and prayed, yet they still have no mate. So instead of asking God for the patience to wait for one he wants for them, they choose Satan's way; God wants the best for you. Please wait on God.

God tells us in his word (Matt. 6:30), "If we seek first the Kingdom of God and his righteousness: ALL things will be added unto us."

As we seek God to cleanse us of the world and help us to become the kind of mate that would be a blessing to someone, we will soon find we are not lonely. First the Lord is using us to bless others, and then we will find that we are content in him. God's plan is to bless us with a *wonderful* mate so that both lives can be witnesses for him. It would be better to remain alone, if we cannot glorify God in our lives.

Chapter Five
SECOND MAJOR CHOICE

Marriage is the second major choice we make in our lives, and we should never enter into it without *prayer*. To rush into a marriage can be disastrous. The most important decision of our lives is the decision to follow *Jesus* . The decision is not a one-time *declaration* but a daily decision to follow *Jesus* above all. If we allow the emotion of our souls' realm to dominate our lives, we are susceptible to the enemy leading us astray. Be careful of Satan's tricks! This area of the flesh should be the Lord's subjection so that Satan does not get advantage and consequently destroy our ministries. So many have failed the Lord because they chose a man or woman over the Lord.

We find this true throughout the Bible too. Solomon's heathen wives led him to idolatry. And a woman, Delilah, turned Sampson from God. Also, David committed murder because of his passion for Bathsheba.

Our emotions need to be cleansed as they are not the sign of love. What's the definition of love if God is not true love? What this world calls love is really built on what the other person does for me, not what I can do for him or her. If the other person does not keep up his or her end of the bargain, a divorce occurs because the offended mate is no longer pleasing the other. This is the attitude of the world's so-called "love."

God's love is love without receiving back; God's love is patient; God's love is gentle and kind; God's love waits; God's love sacrifices.

Chapter Six
MAN'S EMOTIONS

Man's emotions are not a reliable platform upon which to establish a marriage relationship. We need God's spirit to know what God's will is. It is much better to marry for character than for emotion. Emotion changes; character does not. Emotions are in the soul realm, and unless the carnal mind has been renewed with the word of God (Rom. 12:1–2), Satan can and will split up marriages. One of his favorite techniques is to suddenly take away the notion that one still loves one's mate, and then he leads them to divorce, whispering, "You are okay."

After he has destroyed that marriage, he leads one to marry again by stirring one's emotions to another. Often, after the next marriage, something happens that the person does not expect. Before too long, a friction begins to develop with the new mate, then arguing. Finally, they find the same thing happening again. They feel no emotion for the new mate, and the next divorce is in the making. They are falling in Satan's way. The very expression of these words should tell us something. A Christian should not fall for Satan's tricks! And into any trap that Satan sets for us. Love is bigger than simply falling for someone. Certainly, the Lord gives us wonderful emotional feelings for the one we are to marry. However, this feeling without God can be disastrous as Satan can tamper with our emotions and feelings. Marriage in a Christian life should be based on a decision directed by the Holy Spirit. We must rely on the Holy Spirit to direct us in this matter—also all matters of our lives. He knows the future and what is best for us. If we trust him, he will direct our lives (Prov. 3:5–6).

Women and men who allow emotions to rule them will not have victorious Christian lives. Emotions should always follow, never lead.

Chapter Seven
GOD'S LOVE NEVER FAILS

God's love never fails us as does the love of the world. If we are truly seeking God's way, we should believe in God's word. "Be ye not unequally yoked together with unbelievers; for what fellowship does righteousness with unrighteous? And what communion hath light with darkness?" (2 Cor. 6:14). Many precious people suffer because they are living with unsaved mates. Some did know God when they made their marriage decision but have since found Jesus. They will have to pray and love unconditionally to win their mates for Jesus; the Lord always strives to bring the lost mate to him—and the partner who knows him. Mighty miracles of deliverance and salvation have occurred with endured suffering in order to bring their mates to the Lord. Those people who have the light of Jesus marry into darkness by yoking themselves to unsaved mates and find that their flesh has led them out of the will of God.

The Lord wants to bless marriage unions and see his plans fulfilled in both mates' lives. God's plan from the beginning for both male and female is to trust him in this important decisions of life. If we are totally willing to commit to do his will, we will never be disappointed in the ones God sends into our lives.

Chapter Eight
MY PERSONAL STORY

We don't know how God will send our mates to us, but here is my personal story about my mate God sent to me.

I met my mate not in the way I desired to meet him. My brother-in-law had been in prison and now was in a halfway house. My sister called me one day and asked if I would be willing to talk to this guy who was in the halfway house with my brother-in-law. She said that he was a Christian and loved *Jesus*.

Well, of course I agreed to talk with this guy (being the Christian that I am). We began to talk over the phone, and the conversation was about *Jesus* and the Word of God. The anointing of God was over us when we first had our meeting together. Our souls were joined. God knew what he was doing, but we did not at the time. We met in November 2000 and were married in December 2000. (As of today, we have been married twenty years.) I love to tell this story.

God had brought us together. What God was doing was preparing us to do his will. Now he is an associate minister at our church and the prison ministry leader; we go to different prisons and halfway houses to tell the word of God. We are praising God together.

So we have to wait until God puts us with our mates, and we should not be surprised how God does it. I am not telling you to go to the prison to get your mate. What I am telling you is to get instructions from God on what you are to do and where you are to go. Please let the Holy Spirit guide you in the way of God.

As I have said before, the first thing we need to do is seek God and God's way of doing things in our lives. God has the best for us.

Psalm 23

The Lord is my shepherd I shall not be in want

He makes me lie down in green pastures

He restores my soul

Who guides me in the path of righteousness?

for his namesake

even though I walk

Through the Valley of the shadow of death

I will fear no evil

for you are with me

your rod and staff

they comfort me

You prepare a table before me

In the presence of my enemies

You anoint my head with oil

My cup overflows

Surely goodness and love will follow me

All the days of my life

And I will dwell in the house of the Lord, forever

Chapter Nine
LIVING WITH THE MATE GOD GIVES YOU

After you have the mate God wants for you, you need to know how to act in your marriage. Let's look at one of my favor scriptures (Eph. 5:21–33) on marriage.

The first statement tells us to submit to one another from a principle of love to them. the fear of God. What this means is that if we love God, we want what is pleasing to him in all things. We love God so much that all we want to do is pleasing to God.

The Word of God states that the duty of wives is submission to their husbands, including honoring them in the Lord.

The duty of the husbands is to love their wives. The kind of love that Christ has for the church is an example that is sincere, pure, and constant. If we would just obey God's Word and do as the Word states, we could have a marriage that is made in heaven.

This is sense in them, relating to the union between Christ and his church (you and me). There will be failures and defections on both sides, in the present state of human nature. All the duties of marriage are included in unity and love, and while we adore and rejoice in the condescending love of Christ, let the husband and wife learn their duties to each other. The worst evils would be prevented, and many painful effects would be avoided if we could act upon the Word of God in everything that we do.

Christians should take care that all of their behavior answers to their profession. Christians ought to do their duty to one another, from a willing mind and to the obedience to the command of God. Again, wives should be subjects to their husbands, not from dread and amazement but from desire to do well and please God. The husband's duty to the wife implies giving due respect to her and maintaining his authority, protecting her, and placing trust in her. They are heirs together of all blessings of this life and that which comes and should live peaceably, one with another. *Prayer* sweetens their conversation. It is not enough that they pray with family, but husband and wife should pray together by themselves and with their children. Those who are acquainted with prayer find such unspeakable sweetness in it that they will not be hindered therein. I hope that you may pray much and live holy.

We who have entered this godly state of marriage should continue to pray for our marriage and confess that our marriage will grow stronger each and every day in the love of God. When we as Christians do this, we are to show the world how marriage is to be. Read God's Word, study God's Word, and live a godly life. You will have a successful marriage. God bless you and yours.

Marriage Prayer

To love and to cherish,

For better and for worse,

In sickness and in health,

We vow in this verse.

Lord, write on our hearts

This commitment so true,

And love will stay with ours,

Set on you. (Joe and Dorothy Starks)

Printed in the United States
By Bookmasters